D0873824

TALES OF HEAVEN AND EARTH

France Quéré
is a French theologian.
She is the author of
several books about
New Testament women,
Jesus, and the family.

The quotation from the Bible on page 32
is from the King James version.

Cover design by Peter Bennett

Published by Creative Education
123 South Broad Street, Mankato, Minnesota 56001
Creative Education is an imprint
of The Creative Company

Library of Congress Cataloging-in-Publication Data

Quéré, France.
[Celle qui riait quand dieu parlait. English]
Sarah, who loved laughter / by France Quéré;
illustrated by Dorotheé Duntz;
translated by Gwen Marsh.
p. cm. — (Tales of heaven and earth)
Summary: The story of Sarah, wife of Abraham, the
man whom God promised to become father of a nation.
ISBN 0-88682-826-0

1. Sarah (Biblical matriarch)—Juvenile literature.
2. Bible. O.T. Genesis—Biography—Juvenile literature.
[1. Sarah (Biblical matriarch) 2. Bible stories—O.T.]
I. Duntze, Dorothée, ill. II. Marsh, Gwen. III. Title.
IV. Series.
BS580.S25Q4713   1997
222'.11092—dc20   96-30810

6 5 4 3 2 1

Sarah, Who Loved Laughter

by France Quéré

Illustrated by Dorothée Duntze

Translated by Gwen Marsh

 Creative Education

There was no woman more beautiful than Sarai, the wife of Abram.

Chaldea was a region of Mesopotamia. The main town was called Ur. You can see where it was in the map on page 6.

In times long past there lived at Ur in Chaldea a rich peasant. His name was Terah and he had three sons, Abram, Nahor, and Haran.

Haran died young leaving a son, Lot, and two daughters. Nahor was lucky and had twelve boys. Abram, Terah's eldest son, was the last to marry. One would have looked in vain throughout the land for a lovelier woman than his wife, Sarai. But she bore him no children and they both grieved for this. In those times sons remained subject to their father's will. When Terah

Terah was the ninth descendant of Noah, survivor of the Flood. Terah was of the line of Shem, Noah's eldest son, the ancestor of the Semites—people who speak Hebrew, Arabic, or Aramaic.

took it
into his head to
leave Ur and go to
Canaan, a land said to flow with milk
and honey, his family didn't question it. They gathered
their belongings and followed him. The journey was
long, the sun beat down, and Terah, exhausted, finally
gave up. The caravan came to a halt in a town with the
same name as the son he had lost: Haran. Its peaceful
valleys and orchards pleased him and he settled there.

From Ur to Haran, Terah and his family traveled more than 700 miles, but they were still in Mesopotamia. Today the site of Ur is in Iraq and Haran is in Turkey.

His sons set to work again; they sowed,
harvested, and filled their barns. When Terah
died he left them plenty of property. Sarai
worked in the fields and consoled herself for
having no children by playing with the flock of
nephews who were always thronging around her.

One evening Abram returned from the fields excited.
He took his wife aside, "Sarai, I must leave my
father's house, my family, and
this land that I have worked
for heart and soul."

"Who is asking you to
do this?" Sarai was upset.

One day Abram announced to Sarai that God had told them to leave.

"God! God spoke to me! His voice set the sky ablaze and its flames flashed everywhere, even in my heart."

"God? God spoke to you? Where will you go?"

"I shall go wherever he tells me. All I know is, I am leaving."

Sarai went pale. She loved this country, its cradle of hills and the song of the wind in the poplar trees. She looked at Abram with troubled eyes: was he dreaming, like his father? God had only spoken to the first man, Adam, and just one other, Noah. For centuries he had not spoken. Now he was breaking his long silence for this farmer who had no children, whose achievement was measured in vineyards and olive groves. No, this could not be. She opened her mouth to reason with Abram, but he was already outside saddling his donkeys. With a sigh Sarai went in and began folding her clothes.

God in the Bible is heard rather than seen. He speaks into the ears of the prophets and those he has chosen with a voice that can be understood immediately. Sometimes the one he speaks to confuses the voice of God with a human's voice.

7

Abram took with him all that he owned, as if he were leaving forever. Carrying his share of the inheritance, he rode along with his herds, his donkeys, and his servants. His beloved Sarai rode beside him. Some unknown power—the wind, some said—seemed to drive them, and on they went.

God was guiding them toward the smiling land of Canaan, the land their old father had dreamt of but had never seen. Soon their way was lined with hawthorns, alive with swarms of buzzing insects. Abram leaned toward Sarai. God's voice was again in his ear, saying,

Canaan is the name of the land God promised to Abram and his descendants. It extended over the area that is now Israel and Lebanon (see the map on page 6).

. . . and Sarai set off for the land promised by God.

"I shall give this country to your descendants."

A promise of children and a country, or rather a piece of paradise left specially for them on the earth . . . It all sounded too much like a dream. Sarai smiled to herself. But Abram did not smile; he simply gazed up into the azure sky. Twice they stopped along the way and he gathered heavy rocks and built an altar with his bare hands. Sarai watched him. Since he had first told her of God speaking to him he looked different; she hardly recognized him. This close companion of hers held a stranger within him. He roused in her a great sense of astonishment, yet she trusted him. And then there were those sober words always pulsing in her head, "I shall give this country to your posterity."

So they tramped on, over slopes silver with olive trees, up wild rocky solitudes, the haunts of eagles, camping close to villages with fortress walls.

Building an altar meant both paying homage to the divinity and making the place one's own. Abram marked his territory in this way as he traveled south.

"And the Lord appeared unto Abram and said, 'Unto thy posterity I will give this land'; and there builded he an altar unto the Lord, who appeared unto him."
(The Bible, Genesis 12:7)

But worn out and starving, they had to take refuge in Egypt . . .

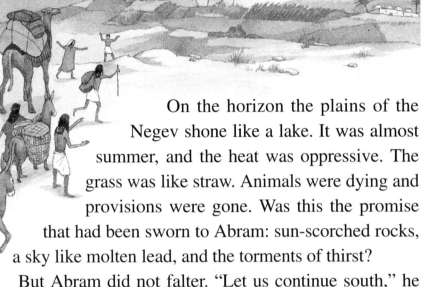

On the horizon the plains of the Negev shone like a lake. It was almost summer, and the heat was oppressive. The grass was like straw. Animals were dying and provisions were gone. Was this the promise that had been sworn to Abram: sun-scorched rocks, a sky like molten lead, and the torments of thirst?

But Abram did not falter. "Let us continue south," he ordered. "Egypt is only a few days away, with fruits and fresh springs of water." They went on, bent with fatigue, and one day they saw, painted on the horizon in green, the end of their ordeal: palm trees, towers, a patchwork of wheatfields and pasture. Abram gripped Sarai's arm. "This country," he said, "is a refuge for us, but it will never be our homeland." He looked at her tenderly, though he was troubled. "Sarai, you are the most beautiful of women. I must expect that some Egyptian will fall in love with you and cut my throat to

Abram's plan was not dictated by personal interest. He was anxious to see God's promise to him fulfilled, and to do so he had to stay alive.

History does not record the name of this pharaoh. He took Sarai into his harem for her beauty but also, perhaps, to learn about her religion.

marry you. Let my sister: that them think that you are way I shall not be an offended rival; they will spare the life of your brother."

He had guessed right. Wherever Sarai passed a murmur of praise was heard. The news of her beauty spread. Pharaoh in his palace would not rest until the young woman was brought to him. When she appeared, he trembled with joy. "She shall be my wife," he declared, and escorted her at once to his apartments. Abram was treated honorably. He was given private gardens, cattle and donkeys groomed as for a festival, and slaves to fan away the flies.

Thus they lived, separately enchained by favors they hated. God in heaven became impatient. Had he chosen Abram just to give pleasure to a heathen? Disasters fell upon the monarch who had snatched God's servant from his mission and his loved one. Hail destroyed the harvest, winds

According to Herodotus, a historian of antiquity, the Egyptians were "the most religious of men." They worshipped a multitude of gods, some of them animals or half human, half animal. Such cults horrified the Hebrews. In their eyes the Egyptians were irreligious and ungodly.

. . . a gilded prison, from which they escaped thanks to God's help.

Jewish tradition interprets Sarai's resignation as the only way to save Abram's life.

blew away the palace roof, the wine in the cellars turned sour, and the pharaoh suffered a mysterious languor which the doctors could not cure.

All this led pharaoh to the truth. He sent for Abram: "Why did you hide from me that Sarai was your wife? Victim of your dishonesty, I believed her to be your sister. I took her into my house. The law gave me the right to do so. Is it fair that I should suffer for a fault I didn't commit?"

Abram hardly listened. God spoke to him in secret and the echo of that voice smothered people's words. But he heard when the pharaoh said, "I cannot punish you: heaven protects you and would strike me without mercy. Take your wife and leave! My soldiers will lead you to the frontier."

Abram could hardly restrain his joy. He had only been waiting for the word of dismissal. Taking Sarai, he roused his slaves, and again they were on the move.

The Jewish faith, and other religions, used to blame some human fault for the misfortunes that befell them, thus God making innocent of the evils suffered by his creatures. What humans endured was the expression of divine justice, so their religious sentiments were not shaken.

Abram was serenity itself. Only one thing concerned him—witnessing the fulfillment of God's promise.

They were returning to Canaan, the land God had promised them.

In desert regions where life depends on finding food for their flocks, people have to be on the move all the time in search of new pastures. These people who wander from place to place like this are called nomads.

They were nomads once more. The first days were an enchantment. They trod the free earth, barefoot. Each morning greeted them with the sight of an infinity of sand wedded to the infinity of sky. The evenings wrapped them in the scarf of the wind. At night they drank the dew of the stars. A blessing hovered over them like a light cloud.

So it was no surprise to Sarai when Abram told her, when they were resting one night, that God had spoken to him again: a voice in the air.

"Has he said anything more about descendants and property?" she asked.

"Do not mock. His voice is like an arch high above the sky. His promises are ten times greater than before. He speaks of multitudes of my descendants and magnificent regions of which I shall be master."

As they went on, the road became very rough. Sarai thought to herself, here we are after months still plodding on at God's command, promise after promise with nothing to show for it, only deserts to cross, rivers and passes to get over—all these ordeals to try our patience! What had they ever gotten from this God who spoke only to her husband and never directly to her?

She kept her doubts entirely to herself, never questioning her husband; but then one day she stole a look at him and caught his eye. She could see the depths of the sky shining there, and his face was strangely lit up. She began to believe that Abram was dwelling in God's truth, and so she took courage. She walked beside him, tired but with steady steps, urged along by the strength of his look and the guiding hand he sometimes laid on her shoulder.

Altogether Abram heard God make seven promises and he endured seven trials, which he came through victoriously. The third promise rewarded him for having given his nephew Lot his independence and a choice of land. The young man chose the well-watered plains of Jordan. Abram took all that remained.

When the town walls of Hebron came into view Abram decreed that they had arrived. They would settle in the country of Mamre nearby. He chose a spot in the shade of an avenue of oak trees where the grass was thick. He drove in his tent pegs and a little way off he made a pile of rocks into his third altar.

The place where Abram set up camp was called Mamre. Tradition puts it two miles to the north of Hebron.

Within a few years he had prospered. His lands extended to the sandy dunes of the desert. He had stores of wine, oil, and wheat. His herds grew vast. He was a good farmer and a wise leader. His soldiers dealt with bandits and drove away invaders. His enemies feared him; his neighbors sought his friendship. He settled disputes, calmed violent tempers. His reputation grew—Abram was powerful yet benign.

Abram conquered huge areas of land and fought off the attacks of neighboring kings who had taken the possessions of his nephew Lot. Abram set Lot free and established peace in the region.

Years passed, carving deep wrinkles into Sarai's lovely face. Her hair grew white. Sometimes Sarai faltered, falling prey to

17

regrets. She said to Abram, "My body is a desert; yours is an army on the march. My soul withers, yet you glow with a breath from high places . . . And I have not been able to make you a father, you whom God has chosen!"

One day when she complained beyond reason he took her hand and gazed up at the night full of stars. "Can you count them—these grains of gold?" he asked her. "God has promised me that the line of my descendants will be numbered like the constellations of stars." Sarai felt encouraged, for his voice had a supernatural gentleness.

Promises are for tomorrow. They drew the old man toward the future. One who looks to a great future remains young. Abram had preserved his strength and stature intact. But Sarai quailed beneath the weight of years. "Too late," she moaned. "I am now the age of a grandmother, not a mother. But time has slipped past my companion without leaving any scars. To him everything is still possible."

Sarai chose not to sit by any longer.

Ten years later, an idea took shape in Sarai's mind: "Why have we been waiting for a child to come? Perhaps God is waiting for us! We have misunderstood each other." She said to Abram, "I'm too old to bear a child. Your descendants can only come from a young woman. Go and find Hagar, my Egyptian servant—she is fifteen. Take her. That is the only way for me to be a mother."

Abram respected Sarai's wish for a child. What she suggested matched his own desire to be a parent, which he had felt for so long. He welcomed the young servant.

Sarai's idea would not have seemed in the least outrageous in those times. Mesopotamian law allowed a barren wife to give her husband a slave so that he would have children to succeed him. The wife could recognize these children as her own.

When Sarai learned that the girl was pregnant she was overjoyed. Alas, not for long! All this had gone to Hagar's head. She felt she was the true mother, as indeed she was; but she also thought she was truly Abram's wife, bound to him by the child of their flesh. As the baby inside her grew she became insolent. She would pass her mistress without a glance, was deaf to her orders, and was soon giving orders herself. Sarai put up with these vexations in silence, but one day she burst out to Abram, "Are you master here or not? Why do you not put this servant in her place? Far from being grateful to me for the honor I have done her, she treats me outrageously, and you—you pretend not to notice!"

Abram had won battles; he had brought justice to the whole country. In order to avoid getting involved in this simple matter, and perhaps too because the great inner voice suggested it, he replied, "She's your servant. Do with her as you wish."

Sarai went back to Hagar and pulled her ears so roughly that the insolent girl took flight into the desert. She had stopped to get her breath when the Angel of the Lord caught up with her. "Where have you come from, young doe, and where are you going?"

Sarai never takes any course of action without asking Abram. Even here, where she is angry with him, she still remains subject to his will.

Hagar instinctively made for the south, the desert, nearer to her native land, Egypt.

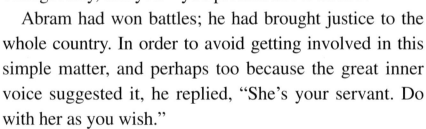

"I am fleeing from my mistress, Sarai."

"Go back at once! Stop playing the haughty princess. You may be a mother, but that gives you no rights. You are a servant and a servant you shall remain."

Hagar felt sad and angry, and the angel softened toward her a little. He told her that she could be proud of her descendants, that they would be numerous. "Give your son the name Ishmael, which means 'God hears.' This will remind you that God took pity on you." Then he added, mysteriously, "Your boy will be a sort of onager. Wild and rebellious, he will hold his own alone against all his brothers. His courage will be your pride."

The servant returned to the fold reluctantly. The birth of Ishmael did little to dispel her resentment.

Thirteen years passed. Abram and Sarai were rich and admired and full of years. The child Ishmael grew tall and strong. While Sarai felt the great evening of life approaching, Abram still kept his youthful vigor. God had not yet kept his promise, yet Abram stood firm, humble, and confident.

He was right. Faith means always believing that life can turn from sorrow to happiness.

"Do you know what God told me this morning, Sarai?"

The onager is an animal that is now extinct. A cross between a donkey and a horse, it was wild and almost untamable. The angel is saying that Ishmael will lead a wandering life in the desert, free and alone.

Abraham was calm and confident that God would keep his promises.

God had said more to Abram. He had promised an eternal alliance with his descendants and ordered circumcision as a sign of that alliance. He had blessed Sarai and announced that she would have a son from whom the promised line would spring.

"No. Tell me."

"He will soon bring about what he has been promising so often these fifty years. And as a sign that this moment is near, he demands that both our names be changed. I shall be Abraham and you will be Sarah."

He stopped and said no more of what God had said.

Abram means the "sublime father" and *Sarai*, "my princess." *Abraham* has the meaning "fertile father" and *Sarah*, "princess for all living beings"— changes to suit the magnificent future awaiting them.

One day three men arrived at Abraham's home.

The noonday heat was like tongues of fire. Abraham was sitting at the entrance to his encampment when he saw three men approaching. He got up and hurried to meet them, offering them hospitality.

While the travelers were resting in the shade of an oak Abraham ran to tell his wife, "Quick, Sarah, take three measures of flour, knead them into flat cakes, and bake them." Then he went out to the field, chose the tenderest calf, and ordered his servant to prepare it at once. When that was done he himself served it with

Abraham performs all the rites of hospitality including washing and providing rest and food. He offers his guests many delicate dishes, undertakes the serving of them himself, standing while his guests eat, and seeing them out when they leave.

They said that Sarah would have a child the next year.

a bowl of curds. He remained standing beside his guests while they were eating.

"Where is your wife, Sarah?" they asked.

"In her tent."

One of the three announced, "She will bear a child. I shall come again next year to visit."

Out of sight, behind the curtain of her tent, Sarah listened. The stranger's words made her burst out laughing: "Me, have a child? My husband and I are two old people. Is this the age for love and for nest making?" Her laughter shook her so much she was almost sobbing.

The visitor frowned. "Why is she laughing? Does she not believe in dawn, in almond trees in bloom, the imperishable youth of the world, and the power of renewal that works in all things on the Earth? Do her wrinkles mean so much to her? There is nothing here on the earth so beautiful that God cannot accomplish it! I say again, meet me in this spot a year from now. Sarah will be nursing her newborn child."

These words changed the parched grass of her distress into a shower of roses. Sarah recognized the voice of God in his messenger. It is never polite to laugh at

These words of the visitor will be uttered again by the angel Gabriel when he tells Mary, the future mother of Jesus, that her cousin Elizabeth, despite her great age, will soon have a son.

visitors, but imagine doubting the word of a spokesman of the most high! Like a child caught misbehaving, she tried to deny it: "No, I wasn't really laughing."

"Yes, Sarah, you were," the stranger said to her, his eyes glinting with mischief. He did not hold it against her, for it was the first time Sarah had heard the Lord speak.

The visitors departed. Abraham saw them on their way. Sarah conceived within the year and in due time bore a lovely boy. Abraham named him Isaac, the child of smiles and laughter. His mother was in her nineties, but old age fell away from her. Her skin became rosy again and her thick hair shone in the moonlight.

The name *Isaac* means "laughter."

They say that laughter brings health. But love brings eternal life. Like every mother, Sarah listened nervously to her baby's slightest cry and was filled with delight when he smiled. Her life was finishing with what should have been its beginning. But who is to say that the mysteries of the world are not like that? You have only to look at the glow of dawn that comes with the dusk.

All her life now, until her last day, was full of childlike gaiety. Sarah's explanation, if anyone wanted to know, was that God had poured his laughter into her heart. "I hear it in my dreams, in the gold of the vines, at dawn when the day is fair, and in the murmuring of the stars."

And everyone who heard her smiled.

Sarah was worried: Would Ishmael try to steal Isaac's inheritance?

The child grew. When he was weaned Abraham gave a banquet. All his friends came. Through the laughter of the party and the clinking of cups, Sarah caught sight of Ishmael picking on little Isaac.

She gave a start. Ishmael, who not so long ago had been the answer to her most fervent prayer, had become a torment to her. She blamed herself for having pushed Hagar into her husband's arms. She was afraid that the adolescent boy might, as eldest, push Isaac to one side and take his inheritance from him. She wanted to be rid of him.

By Hebrew law, the eldest son could inherit from the father, even if born of a concubine.

She leaned close to Abraham. "Drive away this servant and her son! If they remain here they will devour our little Isaac's portion."

Her advice grieved Abraham. Ishmael was his son as much as Isaac. He spent the night in anguished debate with himself. Then God spoke to him in a low voice, "Don't torment yourself, Abraham. Do as Sarah wishes. Her desires suit my hidden design. I shall not abandon your servant's son. He will become the father of a great nation, but it is by Isaac that your descendants will make your name last forever."

Abraham got up. He prepared a bag with provisions and a waterskin of pure water, then he called Hagar and Ishmael. He gave them the provisions, kissed the boy on the forehead, and opened the door. The desert shimmered in the summer heat. Hagar pressed the young boy to her and they walked away quickly. The old man watched as the two shadows were swallowed up in the desert wilderness on their way to Beersheba. Of all the things God commanded him to do, this one broke his heart.

Soon the unhappy woman was plainly lost, the food was eaten, and they were both wracked with thirst. In her

Today Abraham is considered to be the father of those of Jewish, Christian, and Muslim faith.

The desert of Beersheba is to the north of the Negev.

Hagar and her son went into the desert.

despair and sure that both of them would die, she left her son sleeping under a bush and sat down by a pile of rocks, crying. She could not bear to stay and watch her son dying. God heard her weeping. He sent an angel to speak to Hagar: "Stand up, daughter. God has taken pity on your distress! Fetch your child. God shall make him the father of a great nation." Hagar rubbed her eyes, she glimpsed the sparkle of a spring glimmering among the brambles. She filled her waterskin and ran to give it to Ishmael.

God kept them both in the hollow of his hand. Ishmael grew strong and became a hunter and a warrior. He knew where to find water holes, caves, and thorn trees through which animals passed and which became the routes of the camel drivers. His roof was the sky; his walls were spurs of rock.

The Muslims regard as a holy place the spring that God created in the desert to save Ishmael. They visit it when they make the pilgrimage to Mecca. They believe this water, known as *Zemzem*, has healing qualities.

Ishmael had twelve sons; each son was destined to found one of the twelve tribes of the Arabs. It is believed that he lived to be 137 years old.

Sarah, dazzled, beheld in her son the smile of God.

His skill with bows and arrows made him master of the desert. His mother found him an Egyptian wife. He was happy and fathered many children.

At Hebron in the land of Canaan another mother was bringing up another child. Sarah, after all her sadness, had uncovered Abraham's secret and saw in him another greater than he. Now she felt in her own heart a loving presence. She had never been alone, even when she was weary and doubtful; God had touched her with his wings so delicately that she had not known it. Only the look on Abraham's face had given her a hint of that love, only the unshakeable dream that God had put in his head that he would found a nation. It was no longer just a dream; posterity was here, visible in the flesh of her child, the child of her flesh.

According to Jewish tradition, the *Shekhira*, or divine presence, hovered over Sarah's dwelling in the form of a cloud which only disappeared after she died.

Sarah died at Hebron at the age of 127. Abraham acquired the field of Hephron, near Makpela, and buried Sarah there. He joined her in the tomb 38 years later.

31

And he brought him forth abroad,
and said, Look now toward heaven,
and tell the stars, if thou be able to number them:
and he said unto him, So shall thy seed be.
And he believed in the Lord.
Genesis 15:5-6

THE ORIGINS OF SARAH'S STORY

Moses freed his people, the Hebrews, from slavery in Egypt and led them across the desert. On Mount Sinai he received from God the Tables of the Law.

The Bible

The story of Sarah is told in the Bible, the holy book of Jews and Christians. The Bible (from the Greek word *biblia*, meaning books) is written in Hebrew, the ancient language of the Jewish people. It consists of volumes written at different periods (between the 11th and 1st centuries B.C.) and presented in various forms: laws, psalms, histories, prophecies. Christians added to the Jewish Bible another collection of writings called The New Testament. It contains the Gospels, which tell the story of Jesus Christ, and the Epistles, the reports, or testimonies, of his first apostles.

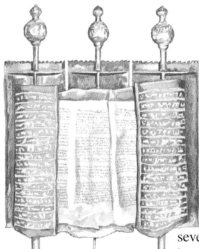

Scroll of the Torah (see page 34)

Genesis

Sarah's story is one of many stories told in Genesis, the first book of the Bible. It has been estimated that these stories were written between the 9th and the 5th centuries B.C. Genesis starts out describing how the world was created in seven days, then it shows how the first two people, Adam and Eve, sinned and were thrown out of paradise. The stories continue to give a chronology of early civilization: the Flood that devastates the Earth, the Tower of Babel that scatters people far and wide.

Toward the end of Genesis, the story of Abraham and Sarah is told to show the lineage of the Hebrews.

The Tower of Babel was inspired by the ziggurats, huge pyramid-shaped towers many flights high, traces of which have been discovered in Mesopotamia. Their stairways seemed to be aimed at heaven itself. That is indeed what men intended with the Tower of Babel. God punished them for their arrogant project by scattering them all over the earth and creating many languages so that they could not understand each other.

SARAH IN THE BIBLE

Sarah is the first of the matriarchs, or great women of the Bible, who had so many wonderful descendants. The story of Sarah as presented in this book tells only a small part of her life.

Judaism (the Jewish religion) looks on Sarah as the mother of the chosen people. "Look unto Abraham your father . . . and unto Sarah that bore you," says the prophet Isaiah in Isaiah 51:2. For Christians, the story of Sarah foreshadows that of the Virgin Mary, who gave birth to Jesus Christ, the founder of their religion.

Women's roles before Sarah

Five thousand years ago, before Sarah's time, there was a cult of mother goddesses. Throughout Mesopotamia and Egypt, in the area where Abraham would roam, women were priests and rulers; they could take several husbands at one time. When such powerful women died, they were buried in elaborate tombs grander than those of men.

However, by Sarah's time, a woman's place had diminished greatly. It was only within the family that women still had great power and authority.

One sentence from Genesis sums up how women came to be viewed: "Eve . . . she was the mother of all living" (Genesis 3:20). In a culture that viewed women's greatest importance as that of being a mother, sterility was the worst of curses.

In the Jewish and Arab world, a man could break the marriage ties and send his wife away for not bearing him a child.

Judaism is founded on the belief in only one God.

Above, a Jewish boy reads the Torah (the first five chapters of the Bible). The text is mounted on two rollers.

The feminine statuettes at the top of this page were found in the coastal region of Canaan. They date from the 8th century B.C. and were offered to Astarte, the goddess of fertility.

Men as patriarchs

As the power of women lessened, men's authority grew much stronger. Men, like Abraham, decided where the family would live and settled money matters and land disputes.

In this story, Abraham has only one legal wife. But his society gives him the right to add concubines to his household, women who might give him children, but who would

Gold and cornelian jewels found in the tomb of a Canaanite woman.

remain subservient to his wife. It is Sarah who suggests that he take Hagar in order to have a child.

Sarah is submissive to Abraham and calls him lord. Even though she handles the servants and determines much of what goes on in the household, Abraham is the head of the family. Abraham rules in matters of religion and politics. It is to Abraham that God speaks.

Women as guardians of the household

Lacking legal and political rights, women concentrated on running household and family affairs. Domestic life depended on them. "Every wise woman buildeth her house: but the foolish plucketh it down with her hands," it says in Proverbs, in the Bible. As did Sarah, women have a decisive influence on their husbands.

Equal in God's eyes

All humans are the same in the eyes of the God of the Bible—men, women, young, old, strangers, and friends. God involves both men and women in his great plans.

Abraham gives in to Sarah because he sees her desire for a child as part of God's will.

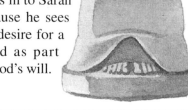

A patriarch in the Bible means the male head of a family.

This head of a woman represents the goddess of fertility, Astarte, worshipped in Canaan. The site of her cult was at Byblos.

Ishtar, the goddess of fertility in Mesopotamia, is shown with a vase that suggests the water of life. (From a sculpture of the third millenium, found at Mari on the Euphrates River.

WHO WAS ABRAHAM?

Top of page:
a ceremony of
offerings before
a small altar,
from a bronze
of the 12th
century B.C. that
comes from Susa
(Mesopotamia).

Below, left,
a king carrying
a lamb as
an offering
to a god.

A person
praying to a god,
from a bronze
of the 18th
century B.C.

This carving from Mesopotamia represents a female musician of the time of Abraham.

The time of Abraham

For the Hebrews, Abraham is their ultimate father, the source of their lineage. The Bible sets him in the immeasurable depths of time, ten generations after the Flood. Some historians think he lived at the time of the kings (10th century B.C.), some at the return from exile (400 years later), some much earlier—about 1800 years B.C.

The setting of this story

If the Bible is unspecific about setting Abraham in time, it is more helpful about place (see page 6). We know that Abraham was born in the town of Ur in Mesopotamia. The area he was born in is now part of the country of Iraq. He traveled with Sarah through the Middle East, in what we now call Israel and Lebanon.

The towns of Ur and Haran have some features in common: both were fertile plains, both were prosperous trading centers where major travel routes crossed. Religious cults there were devoted to the same lunar divinities: the god Sin and the goddess Nin-Gal, borrowed from Sumerian mythology.

Abraham's faith

Abraham lived in an idolatrous land, both polytheistic (worshipping many gods) and animist (making gods of natural forces). He obeyed an inner voice promising him a great nation. As Abraham traveled, he built altars along his route, as many nomads would, to claim new territories, but also as an act of faith—it was his way of spreading the cult of the one god. This new culture of the Hebrews challenged the declining gods and goddesses and the social customs of the surrounding civilizations.

Top of page:
Banner of Ur,
a wooden panel
of which one
side evokes war
(above, battle of
chariots), and
the other side
evokes peace (a
banquet scene).
These two
themes are also
associated on the
ivory plaque
(below) from
Megiddo, in
Canaan.

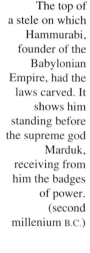

The top of
a stele on which
Hammurabi,
founder of the
Babylonian
Empire, had the
laws carved. It
shows him
standing before
the supreme god
Marduk,
receiving from
him the badges
of power.
(second
millenium B.C.)

According to the
Bible, there is a
sanctuary (right)
above the cave
near Hebron
where Sarah was
buried. Abraham
is also said to lie
there, with his
son Isaac and his
grandson Jacob.

How to establish a new nation

The book of Genesis tells of how Abraham's family took part in setting up a new nation: the men by their military conquests, the women by their fertility and their commitment to the line of God's chosen people.

Against this background we must understand Sarah's jealousy of Ishmael, the son of the Egyptian Hagar. Sarah wanted her own child to further God's plan. Like Abraham she helped to form the covenant made between God and humankind. A text from the time of the first Christians, part of the Epistle to the Hebrews, praises Sarah for her faith: "Through faith also Sarah herself received strength to conceive seed, and was delivered of a child when she was past age, because she continued faithful to Him who had promised." (Hebrews 11:11).

Abraham's connection to God

With Abraham, direct communication between God and man took on more importance, as if humanity were growing up. God made demands so extreme that they were difficult to understand: "Leave your country, your parents, your father's house, and go to the land I shall show you."

Abraham had no idea what his wanderings meant, nor to where they would lead him. His obedience to God was written in his heart long before it was the first commandment in the Table of Moses (see page 33): "Thou shalt love the Lord thy God with all thy heart, with all thy soul,

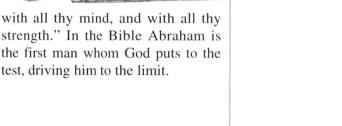

with all thy mind, and with all thy strength." In the Bible Abraham is the first man whom God puts to the test, driving him to the limit.

ONE GOD

The picture here shows the statue of the god (on the far left) worshipped in the little temple of Hazor (Canaan), of the 14th century B.C., with votive steles that mark the making or granting of a vow or wish.

Among the desert peoples that we know of, only the Hebrews did not worship a number of gods (see page 36). Thanks to the messages of their prophets, they kept their belief in the one god.

A religion born of a nomadic life

The Hebrews, with their wandering, nomadic lifestyle, could not tie their rites to particular places or fixed objects such as trees, rocks, wells, let alone towns. In Chaldea, for instance, each town had its own god to protect it. So, for lack of a fixed place of worship, Hebrews came to believe in a god who was always with them, present wherever they went. The Bible shows Abraham, though part of a polytheistic culture, worshipping one God. The Hebrews followed Abraham, to become the first monotheistic people.

The God of Abraham

Other divinities are local—the God of the Hebrews is universal. He goes well beyond the specialities of other divinities—the universe is his work.

Top of page: Statuettes of worshippers, in alabaster with eyes encrusted with lapis-lazuli gems, from Mesopotamia (the Iraq of today), from the third millenium B.C.

Cattle rearing was the main livelihood of the nomadic Hebrew people and especially of such patriarchs as Abraham. (After an Egyptian fresco of the 14th century B.C.)

His relationship with the Hebrew people forms a holy story with a universal importance. God manifests himself through covenants, promises, laws, and alliances, which are seen by the Hebrew people as proofs of love.

A God without a name

Abraham probably did use a name to address God, but the authors of the Bible chose to use a string of unpronounceable letters to signify God's name. This was a mark of respect for God and showed that God cannot be compared to anything on Earth, or even be represented—his very name cannot be pronounced.

A God of mercy

The God of Abraham revealed in the Bible does not want human sacrifices, which were not uncommon during the time. As a test of his servant's faith, God asks Abraham to kill his son Isaac and offer him on an altar. Abraham is ready to do it, when God intervenes and tells him to "lay down the knife." His son is saved.

Abraham believes his God is close by, easy to talk to. The God of the Bible is Abraham's friend, counselor, and protector.

Two parallel stories

In the Bible, two stories are told side by side. One story is the revelation of the God of the Hebrews. The other story shows mankind growing up and acquiring the ability to make a choice.

Baal, god of the storm, holds the lightning and the axe (left). He also stands on a lion, symbol of the natural forces that he rules.

Below, a Phoenician censer in bronze and a zither player.

Look for other titles in this series:

THE SECRETS OF KAIDARA
An Animist Tale from Africa

I WANT TO TALK TO GOD
A Tale from Islam

THE RIVER GODDESS
A Tale from Hinduism

CHILDREN OF THE MOON
Yanomami Legends

I'LL TELL YOU A STORY
Tales from Judaism

THE PRINCE WHO BECAME A BEGGAR
A Buddhist Tale

JESUS SAT DOWN AND SAID . . .
The Parables of Jesus